8/16/07

P9-CDA-509

Amazon Journey

Amazon
Journey

Cruising the Rain Forest

By Gare Thompson

NATIONAL GEOGRAPHIC

WASHINGTON D.C.

One of the world's largest nonprofit scientific and educational organizations, the National Geographic Society was founded in 1888 "for the increase and diffusion of geographic knowledge." Fulfilling this mission, the Society educates and inspires millions every day through its magazines, books, television programs, videos, maps and atlases, research grants, the National Geographic Bee, teacher workshops, and innovative classroom materials. The Society is supported through membership dues, charitable gifts, and income from the sale of its educational products. This support is vital to National Geographic's mission to increase global understanding and promote conservation of our planet through exploration, research, and education.

For more information, please call
1-800-NGS-LINE (647-5463) or write to the following address:
National Geographic Society
1145 17th Street N.W.
Washington, D.C. 20036-4688
U.S.A.

For information about special discounts for bulk purchases, please contact
National Geographic Books Special Sales at ngspecsales@ngs.org

Visit the Society's Web site: www.nationalgeographic.com

Published by National Geographic Society. Washington, D.C. 20036

Design by Project Design Company

Printed in the United States

Library of Congress Cataloging-in-Publication Data

Thompson, Gare.
   Amazon journey : cruising the rain forest / by Gare Thompson.
      p. cm. -- (National Geographic science chapters)
   Includes bibliographical references and index.
   ISBN-13: 978-0-7922-5951-0 (library binding)
   ISBN-10: 0-7922-5951-3 (library binding)
   1. Amazon River Region--Description and travel. I. Title. II. Series.
   F2517.T47 2006
   918.1'10465--dc22

   2006016320

Photo Credits
Front Cover: © David Tipling/ Getty Images; Spine: © J. P. Fruchet/ Getty Images; Endpaper: © J. P. Fruchet/ Getty Images; 2-3: © Claire Leimbach/ Robert Harding World Imagery/ Getty Images; 6: © Michael Nichols/ National Geographic Image Collection; 8: © Wolfgang Kaehler/ Corbis; 10: © ANT Photo Library; 11: © Nick Caloyianis/ National Geographic Image Collection; 12-13: © Jacques Jangoux/ Auscape; 14: © Nicolas Raynard/ National Geographic Image Collection; 15: © Pete Oxford/ naturepl.com; 16: © ANT Photo Library; 17: © Jason Edwards/ Bio-Images; 19: © Corbis; 20: © Stephen G. St. John/ National Geographic Image Collection; 22-23: © Michael Nichols/ National Geographic Image Collection; 24: © Theo Allofs/ zefa/ Corbis; 25: © National Geographic/ Getty Images; 26: © Jacques Jangoux/ Auscape; 27: © S. Gutierrez-Explorer/ Auscape; 29 (bottom): © Anisio Magalhaes/ SambaPhoto/ Getty Images; 29 (top): © Joe MacDonald/ Auscape; 30: © Martin Harvey/ Corbis; 32: © Acclaim Images; 33: © Erwin & Peggy Bauer/ Auscape; 34: © Getty Images; 35: © Erik Sampers/ Stock Image/ Getty Images; Map by National Geographic Maps.

Contents

The Amazon River winds its way
through the rain forest in Brazil.

The Amazon River

Let's travel the second longest river in the world. The Amazon River is about 4,000 miles (6,440 km) long. It flows across the northern part of South America.

Our trip will take us deep into the heart of the world's largest rain forest. Pack your camera. You don't want to miss taking photos of the wonderful sights we'll see.

It rains a lot where we are going. So bring rain gear and a waterproof sleeping bag. Pack light clothes. Most of the time the air is hot and humid. Light clothes will dry out faster. Ready? Let's go!

People shop in the market in Belém, Brazil.

Chapter 1

Starting Out: Belém

We are in the city of Belém, in Brazil. It is at the mouth of the mighty Amazon River. The mouth of a river is the place where the river empties into a large body of water. At Belém, the Amazon fans out to join the Atlantic Ocean.

No other river pours out as much water as the Amazon. More than 1,000 other rivers flow into the Amazon. Some parts of the river run fast. The currents can be strong and dangerous.

A Museum Tour

Before we get on our boat, let's go into a museum. The museum has a zoo, a garden, and a research center. Here we will see and feel what the rain forest will be like.

Inside, insects called cicadas are making a loud buzzing noise. Our guide tells us cicadas are just one kind of insect we'll find in the rain forest. Millions of different kinds of bugs live in the rain forest. It's a good thing I like bugs.

Like other rodents, an agouti eats plants.

One kind of manatee makes its home in the Amazon River.

I almost step on an agouti. It is a large rodent. Yuck! The guide reminds me that that I will have to watch where I walk, sit, and lean in the forest. I don't want to sit on a snake or scorpion!

We see a manatee. It is also called a sea cow. It swims in the water. We also see a harpy eagle. It is the strongest bird of prey in the world. It is amazing.

People sell pots and other goods at the market in Belém.

The Harbor

Belém is a busy harbor city. We stop at the fish market. You can find all kinds of fish here. The fish come from the Amazon River. It has more kinds of fish living in it than any other river. People sell piranha, a flesh-eating fish. They also sell surubim, a long-nosed, striped catfish. It is funny looking, but it tastes good. Walking around the market is like being inside an aquarium.

People sell more than fish in the harbor.
Boats deliver all kinds of goods. There are
tables of fruits that are grown along the river.
Like in other markets, pottery and clothes are
also for sale. There are plants for sale, too.

We will sail from Belém up the river. Over
the next six days we'll sail about 1,000 miles
(1,610 km) to the next major city, Manaus.
On the way we will stop and explore some of
the tributaries that flow into the Amazon.

Soil in the water makes
the river look brown.

Chapter 2

Up the River

Our boat is a large cruise ship. The guide tells us more about the river. Some parts of the Amazon look brown and muddy. That's because the water is carrying soil, called sediment.

We see a pink dolphin swimming in the river. These freshwater dolphins are born gray, but turn pink as they get older. It looks like a splash of pink paint against a dark canvas.

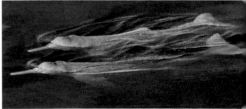

Pink dolphins swim in the Amazon River.

A basilisk has flaps on its toes that enable it to run on top of the water.

Later, we see a small lizard called a basilisk. I use my binoculars to look at it. It runs across the water on its back legs. It is funny to see the basilisk running across the water.

At night the river is noisy. The bugs, the birds, and the noise of the river itself finally lull me to sleep. It is still hot at night. We sleep with bug nets over our hammocks. The bugs do not seem to sleep.

Exploring a Small River

It is early morning. The sun is bright. It is hot and humid. Our guide tells us to bring our rain gear because it will rain later. It rains here almost every day. That is why many parts of the river are so deep.

We leave the ship and travel in a small boat up a small river that flows into the Amazon. The water moves faster in the smaller river than on the Amazon. The guide controls the boat. It is hard work.

Only small boats can travel on the smaller rivers that flow into the Amazon.

A macaw perches on a tree branch.

We find a spot to stop. The guide warns us to be alert as we explore. We must also stay together. The air is damp. After a few minutes we are all wet. Then I see a magical sight. It is a beautiful, blue butterfly called a morpho. Our guide tells us that airplane pilots see these amazing butterflies as they fly over the river. The butterfly shimmers in the light. The guide says that morpho butterflies are easy to see but very hard to catch.

Trees hang over us. The guide points out the many layers of plants in the forest. The plants fight for sunlight. Different birds and animals live at each layer. Suddenly a macaw swoops by. It looks like a flying rainbow. It is brightly colored. It has a powerful beak to break nuts. It is the largest of all parrots.

We make our way back to the boat. I watch out for bugs. They seem to be everywhere.

Morpho butterflies spend most of their time in the lower levels of the rain forest.

Boats are loaded with goods in Manaus.

Chapter 3

Docking in Manaus

After six days on the boat, we dock in Manaus. The port is filled with boats. There are cruise ships filled with people. There are fishing boats full of fish. And there are boats filled with other kinds of goods. The Amazon is like a highway. But instead of cars and trucks, there are boats.

Our guide tells us about the city. In the 1890s, Manaus was the "king" of the rubber trade. Rubber trees grew around the city. There were many plantations, or large rubber farms. Ships carried the rubber down the Amazon.

A local man cuts slits in the bark of a rubber tree in order to collect the sap that is used to make rubber.

By the early 1900s, Manaus was one of the richest cities in the Americas. Ships came to Manaus from all over the world. But then rubber production moved to the Far East. Many people left Manaus.

Today, tourists visit Manaus. People living here work in hotels and restaurants. Others sell goods to the tourists. After

being on the boat so long, it is nice to be in
a city and to sleep in a bed.

Manaus is on the bank of the Rio Negro.
We decide to explore this river that runs
into the Amazon. The Rio Negro is almost
black. It is dark because the leaves in the
river turn the water dark. They stain the
water like tea.

In this shallow part, the river looks like a green carpet. The green carpet turns out to be huge water lilies. These water lilies are about 6 feet (2 m) across! A small child can float on them! We finally get past them and spot more fish.

Giant water lilies float on the top of the river.

Piranhas have razor-sharp teeth.

We see a school of red piranha. The guide tells us to keep our hands in the boat. These fish can tear a large animal to bits in minutes. I sit on my hands.

Slowly we make our way back to the city. We will make one more stop in our large ship. Then we have to travel by canoe. It is the only way to get closer to the source, or the beginning, of the Amazon River.

Families live along the banks of the Amazon.

Chapter 4

Visiting a River Village

After ten days, we dock in Iquitos, Peru. From here we must travel by canoe. Parts of the river are not deep enough for big boats. In other places the river narrows and is filled with jagged rocks. We get into our canoe and wave goodbye to the people on the dock.

Villagers use canoes to travel up and down the river.

Now it seems like we are entering the heart of the river. The river flows faster here. The guide watches for rocks and narrow passages. It is easy to tip the canoe over in the fast rapids. We wear life jackets.

We are going deeper into the forest as we travel up the river. Along the river are small towns and villages. The people wave. Some of the villages have schools and other buildings. We move still deeper into the forest. The villages are getting farther from the river banks.

As we travel on, it seems like we are moving back in time. We stop at one village. It is in a clearing in the forest. The guide tells us to follow him and do as he does.

The villagers have lived here for hundreds of years. They live today like they did long ago. All the people in the village share their things. They use blowguns to hunt for food. Darts are tipped with poison from a vine.

A villager hunts with a blowgun.

◀ Boys hunt in the forest with bows and arrows.

We see some men coming back from fishing. They do not use fishing poles. Instead, they use a poison made from the barbasco plant. The men pour it into the river. It stuns the fish. Then they wade in and collect the fish.

Chapter 5

Into the
Rain Forest

From the air, the rain forest looks like a giant green blanket. But it has layers, and each layer is different.

The ground layer is the forest floor. It is full of wet leaves. Insects of all kinds seem to be crawling everywhere.

The next level is the understory. Green plants hang down like ropes. Big snakes wind around the branches.

The next level looks like a large umbrella. It is called the canopy. Here is where we see parrots flying and spider monkeys swinging

Many different kinds of plants grow in the rain forest.

A jaguar rests in a tree.

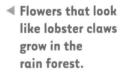

◀ Flowers that look
like lobster claws
grow in the
rain forest.

on the vines. There are sloths hanging upside
down by their three toes.

The top level is called the emergent level.
Here tall trees stick out. Harpy eagles nest
here. They seem to guard the forest.

Amazing Plants and Animals

I see something that looks like a lobster's claw, but it's a flower. The guide says there are 450 kinds of this flower here. They look like lobsters hanging from the trees. These flowers love the hot, damp climate of the rain forest.

The guide holds up his hand. There is a jaguar. It is the "king" of the Amazon. It is the biggest cat in the forest. This one is sleeping in a tree. We move away quietly.

Suddenly we spot squirrel monkeys. There are about 30 of them. They chatter and swing quickly around. I'm not afraid of them.

Then I see a scorpion sitting on the tree next to me. The scorpion does scare me. I'm glad I was paying attention. I almost put my hand there! I see an iguana scurry away. Too bad they are so shy. I'd like to see one up close.

A sloth hangs from a tree branch.

The amazing Amazon River cuts across most of South America.

The Source of the Amazon

It's impossible to reach the source of the Amazon by boat. The river gets narrower and narrower as it gets closer to its source high in the Andes Mountains. There, water from a small lake flows down from the mountain. Other streams flow into it until it builds to the mighty Amazon.

The Amazon is an amazing river. There are still many parts left to explore. There are many more strange plants and animals to see. I'm already planning my next trip. Want to come along?

How to Write an A+ Report

1. Choose a topic.
- Find something that interests you.
- Make sure it is not too big or too small.

2. Find sources.
- Ask your librarian for help.
- Use many different sources: books, magazine articles, and websites.

3. Gather information.
- Take notes. Write down the big ideas and interesting details.
- Use your own words.

4. Organize information.
- Sort your notes into groups that make sense.

- Make an outline. Put your groups of notes in the order you want to write your report.

5. Write your report.

- Write an introduction that tells what the report is about.

- Use your outline and notes as you write to make sure you say everything you want to say in the order you want to say it.

- Write an ending that tells about your report.

- Write a title.

6. Revise and edit your report.

- Read your report to make sure it makes sense.

- Read it again to check spelling, punctuation, and grammar.

7. Hand in your report!

Glossary

bank	the land along each side of the river
canopy	the level of a rain forest between the understory and the emergent level
current	the flow of water
emergent level	the top level of a rain forest
forest floor	the bottom level, or floor, of a rain forest
mouth	the place where a river empties into a large body of water
plantation	a large farm
port	a place where ships can dock to load and unload goods
rain forest	an area with many tall trees that gets large amounts of rain each year
rapids	parts of a river where the currents are fast
sediment	materials such as the sand, clay, and rock that are carried by a river
source	the place where a river starts
tributary	a stream that flows into a river
understory	the level of a rain forest between the forest floor and the canopy

Further Reading

• Books •

Barter, James. *The Amazon (Rivers of the World)*. San Diego, CA: Lucent Books, 2003. Ages 10-14, 112 pages.

Chapman, Simon. *Explorers Wanted:! In the Jungle*. New York, NY: Little, Brown, and Company, 2005. Ages 9-12, 128 pages.

Fitzpatrick, Anne. *The Amazon River (Natural Wonders of the World)*. Mankato, MN: Creative Education, 2005. Ages 9-12, 32 pages.

Graf, Mike. *The Amazon River*. Mankato, MN: Capstone Press, 2003. Ages 9-12, 32 pages.

Grupper, Jonathan. *Destination: Rain Forest*. Washington, DC: National Geographic Society, 1997. Ages 8-10, 32 pages.

• Websites •

Kidzworld
http://www.kidzworld.com/site/p3178.htm

National Geographic Society
http://www.nationalgeographic.com/wildworld/profiles/g200/g147.html

Passport to Knowledge
http://passporttoknowledge.com/rainforest/intro.html

Public Broadcasting Service
http://www.pbs.org/journeyintoamazonia/about.html

ThinkQuest
http://library.thinkquest.org/21395/

Wikipedia Online Encyclopedia
http://en.wikipedia.org/wiki/Amazon_river/

World Rainforest Information Portal
http://www.rainforestweb.org/

Index